BIG
DOGS

IRISH WOLFHOUNDS

by Allan Morey

Content Consultant: Sarah K. Crain
Doctor of Veterinary Medicine
Tufts University
North Grafton, Massachusetts

Pebble
Plus

CAPSTONE PRESS
a capstone imprint

Pebble Plus is published by Capstone Press,
1710 Roe Crest Drive, North Mankato, Minnesota 56003
www.mycapstone.com

Library of Congress Cataloging-in-Publication Data
Names: Morey, Allan, author.
Title: Irish wolfhounds / by Allan Morey.
Description: North Mankato, Minnesota : Capstone Press, a Capstone imprint,
  2016. | ?2016 | Series: Big dogs | Audience: Ages 5-7.? | Audience: K to
  grade 3.? | Includes bibliographical references and index.
Identifiers: LCCN 2015030280 | ISBN 9781491479810 (library binding)
Subjects: LCSH: Irish wolfhound--Juvenile literature. | Dog breeds--Juvenile
  literature.
Classification: LCC SF429.I85 M67 2016 | DDC 636.753/5--dc23
LC record available at http://lccn.loc.gov/2015030280

Editorial Credits
Nikki Bruno Clapper, editor; Juliette Peters, designer;
Morgan Walters, media researcher; Katy LaVigne, production specialist

Photo Credits
Dreamstime: Tatiana Belova, 13, Veronika Druk, 9; Getty Images: Robert Daly, 11, 17; Newscom:
Patrick Pleul/dpa/picture-alliance, 19; Shutterstock: ARTSILENSE, 1, andrewvec, (speedometer)
cover, CaseyMartin, 7, DragoNika, 15, Eric Isselee, (dog) bottom left 22, Hywit Dimyadi, (dog
silouette) cover, Jolanta Beinarovica, cover, kostolom3000, (dog head) backcover, 3, Marcel Jancovic,
5, nancy dressel, 21, Stephaniellen, (elephant) bottom right 22, vlastas, (paw prints) design element
throughout

Note to Parents and Teachers

The Big Dogs set supports national science standards related to life science. This book describes
and illustrates Irish wolfhounds. The images support early readers in understanding the text. The
repetition of words and phrases helps early readers learn new words. This book also introduces
early readers to subject-specific vocabulary words, which are defined in the Glossary section. Early
readers may need assistance to read some words and to use the Table of Contents, Glossary, Read
More, Internet Sites, Critical Thinking Using the Common Core, and Index sections of the book.

Printed in the United States of America in North Mankato, Minnesota.
102015   009221CGS16

Table of Contents

THE TALLEST DOG

The Irish wolfhound
is the tallest dog breed.
These dogs are slim
and trim. They are
built for speed!

Irish wolfhounds are
a type of hound dog.
They were bred as hunters.
They chased big animals
like boars and elk.

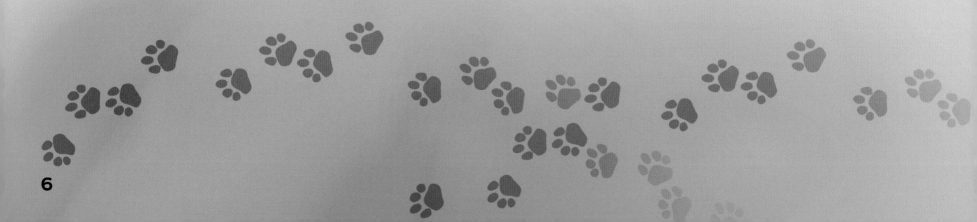

LONG AND GRACEFUL

Irish wolfhounds have long, thin bodies. They need soft places to rest. Beds and couches are their favorites!

Irish wolfhounds are huge
but graceful. Big dogs
have shorter lives than small
dogs do. Wolfhounds live
for only 6 to 8 years.

CARING FOR AN IRISH WOLFHOUND

Irish wolfhounds need good training. Puppies like to chew on shoes and furniture. They must learn to behave.

Irish wolfhounds still
have a chasing instinct.
They are gentle with people.
But sometimes they chase
other pets and wild animals.

Irish wolfhounds are
"counter surfers." They are
tall enough to grab food off
a counter! Training helps
them leave food alone.

Irish wolfhounds need a lot
of exercise. These dogs
need long walks and
playtime each day.

Big dogs need a lot of care.
But Irish wolfhounds are
sweet, loving dogs. They can
be great family pets.

GLOSSARY

behave—to act properly

boar—a wild pig

breed—a certain kind of animal within an animal group; to mate and produce young

elk—a large deer with big, curved antlers

exercise—a physical activity done in order to stay healthy and fit

gentle—kind and calm

hound—a type of dog that is often trained to hunt

instinct—behavior that is natural rather than learned

training—teaching an animal to do what you say

HOW BIG ARE THEY?

	Irish Wolfhound	Baby Elephant
Average Height	30–34 inches (76–86 centimeters)	36 inches (91 cm)
Average Weight	105–150 pounds (48–68 kilograms)	200 pounds (91 kg)

42
36
30
24
18
12
6
0

READ MORE

Graubart, Norman D. *My Dog.* Pets Are Awesome! New York: PowerKids Press, 2014.

Landau, Elaine. *Irish Wolfhounds Are the Best!* The Best Dogs Ever. Minneapolis, Minn.: Lerner Publications, 2011.

Rajczak, Kristen. *Irish Wolfhounds.* Great Big Dogs. New York: Gareth Stevens Pub., 2012.

INTERNET SITES

FactHound offers a safe, fun way to find Internet sites related to this book. All of the sites on FactHound have been researched by our staff.

Here's all you do:

Visit *www.facthound.com*

Type in this code: 9781491479810

Super-cool stuff!
Check out projects, games and lots more at
www.capstonekids.com

CRITICAL THINKING USING THE COMMON CORE

1. Irish wolfhounds are known as "counter surfers." What does this mean? (Key Ideas and Details)

2. Irish wolfhounds were bred as hunters. How might you keep them from chasing small animals in the park? (Integration of Knowledge and Ideas)

INDEX